Gavin Bone

Anglo-Saxon Poetry

AN ESSAY

WITH SPECIMEN TRANSLATIONS
IN VERSE

BY

GAVIN DAVID BONE

Late Fellow and Tutor of St. John's College,
Oxford

 BOOKS FOR LIBRARIES PRESS
FREEPORT, NEW YORK

First published 1943 by Oxford University Press, Inc.

Reprinted 1970 by arrangement

INTERNATIONAL STANDARD BOOK NUMBER:

0-8369-5494-7

LIBRARY OF CONGRESS CATALOG CARD NUMBER:

75-128874

PRINTED IN THE UNITED STATES OF AMERICA

THE HAPPY LAND

I have heard   there is hence
Far away   from the world
A nook in the East,   a noble plain,
Great, and girt   with gallant trees,
Which the Lord   from living men
Has shut tight,   shielded quite,
Since he formed   first the world.
That victorious plain   pleasant shall remain,
With no pain   and no rain,
No showers to steep,   no rime to creep,
No hot sky,   no screaming hail;
Always the plain   is a pleasant place.
For there are no mountains   high and proud,
Nor any stone cliffs,   starving clefts,
Precipices leaning up,   precipices leaning down,
But the noble plain   never fails to stand
Even and open,   unanxiously perfect.
That bright bower   does bravely tower
Ten times as high   as the tallest hill,
Which white and bright   gives the world light
And shines to men   under the shining of the stars.

From 'THE PHOENIX'

Preface

THE short essay which accompanies the translations of Anglo-Saxon poems was never completed nor revised by its author who died in 1942. It remains, as it were, merely the opening paragraph of a longer work he had planned upon Anglo-Saxon poetry as a part of the main fabric of English literature. One other chapter—upon the epic poem *Beowulf*—was written; and this, with the author's version of the poem itself, may be printed later. It is considered that the present essay suggests enough of the author's purpose to justify its inclusion here.

He felt, that while there has been a continuous body of English literature for twelve centuries; from the eighth to the tenth no other European language could offer anything of such variety, extent, or finish, as the Anglo-Saxon verse of that period;—verse written for a class of some culture and with a high degree of sophistication. He believed that because of the later and more widely studied influences of the Celtic, French, and Classical sources upon English literature, the importance of the native stock had been underestimated,—that native stock which despite some arid stretches of versification seemed to him full of sap and vigour. As a scholar, the cragginess and difficulty of the language attracted him, and as an artist he delighted in the elaborate technique of Anglo-Saxon alliterative verse.

In his translation of the poems into English verse, he wished to convey to the modern reader the same kind of pleasure which he himself had derived from his reading of the Anglo-Saxon. For this he chose a very free rendering of the text, considering that a loitering over or teasing of the language would defeat his purpose. His choice of poems for translation indicates the trend of his meaning, for such poems were chosen as are distinctively Anglo-Saxon in character and spirit. His feeling for what is vital and of interest to the modern reader is confirmed by the first and last poems translated. The *Battle of Maldon* (which is here placed first though actually the latest in date) was written after the defeat of the Saxons by the Danes, A.D. 991, at Maldon in Essex, in the darkest days of the Danish invasions when Ethelred the Unready was King. In this poem occur the famous lines:—

> The will shall be harder, the courage shall be keener
> Spirit shall grow great, as our strength falls away.

The last poem, much earlier in date, where the poet muses upon the ruins of the Roman city of Bath, shows the persistent elegiac mood in Anglo-Saxon poetry.

G. H. B.

Contents

Introduction

'WHEN the South wind troubles grimly the gentle sea, grey and clear as glass, then great waves disturb it, they beat up the whale's pool—rough is then what before was glad to look on.'

So does King Alfred translate the Latin of Boethius into his verses—a humdrum task until this 'Whale's pool' inserts itself into the translation. It is quite unwarranted. It is padding, but it is nevertheless arresting. It brings us in a flash from Italy and Boethius's Mediterranean (where the South Wind is the troubler) to the seas of the North As I read it over one day I thought I would inquire farther. Surely there is confusion. The South Wind does not trouble us here. The Whale's pool is in our Northern seas. Sure enough, the phrase has edged its way in and imposed itself upon the Latin, which runs: 'When the violent South wind, moving the sea, churns up the billows, the wave, but now glassy and clear as day, soon catches the eye, foul with ooze dissolved.' It is an unwarrantable piece of pictorial padding, that Whale's pool, but it shows what its author thinks will be automatically acceptable to his readers with little trouble to himself. It has always been found to work and he supposes, always will. Something for effect which costs little labour.

The Whale's pool then, represents what Anglo-Saxon poetry knows it can do well. Consider Virgil, who, when he feels himself becoming dull, introduces something about serpents. He knows he can make an effect there. Milton introduces something about astronomy—he may get his astronomy wrong, saying that Ophiucus is in the Arctic sky, or that the Great Bear sets, but he has his effect. Now the 'Whale's pool' provides something of an answer to those who inquire whether Anglo-Saxon poetry has any unique quality, whether there is any reason why it should be studied.

When the reader is informed that there are thirty thousand lines of Anglo-Saxon poetry extant, he wants to know whether there is very much in the great collections of which he has heard—the Exeter Book, the Vercelli Book, the Cædmon or the *Beowulf* manuscript—which will give him a kind of poetry which he does not know at all.

In a general way, he knows of the Greek poets and cannot escape Homer. He knows of the Psalms; he knows perhaps of Chinese poetry and the moment of insight when the moon looks at one or one has failed in an examination. About the latter he may remark, 'How modern!' But when his attention is directed to Anglo-Saxon poetry he demands to know, 'Is it different?'

Let us begin by considering the qualities which all poetry shares. Perhaps the great poets were the inventors of phrases, and perhaps it was they who found rich veins of material. But however a poetical tradition begins, a common stock is soon arrived at. All the lesser poets fasten on the stock, add to it very little, but draw on it for all their effects, seeking always for variety, but (as it seems to later times) leaving behind them a mass of poetry in which the qualities displayed in common are very numerous compared with those peculiar to each poet. Much in the same way all tunes on the bagpipes sound the same to an Englishman. That there is a very obvious common heritage is particularly true in Anglo-Saxon poetry. The poets 'lift' from each other cheerfully. Generally they vary the phrase in the process. We find that the 'Whale's pool' becomes a variation of 'Whale's road'. Anything of that kind will do! There is 'Gannet's Bath'. These are the common stock. These are not like any poetry which the reader is likely to know.

The first unusual fact which imposes itself on the student of Anglo-Saxon poetry is the portmanteau descriptive phrase: an attempt to include in the name of a thing as much as possible of the thing itself. It is, of course, an eternal effort of the poets to seize as much as possible in a single hug. Blood-boltered Banquo is before us. The Anglo-Saxons would try again. Macbeth would be the battle-young king, the loathed people-pillager.

Calling names is one excellence of Anglo-Saxon poets, but they are not limited to bad names. They draw upon a wonderful stock of epithets when they describe their second country the sea—that Gannet's Bath, that Whale's Road, that Swan's Path—and even in the most ordinary Anglo-Saxon poetry the method produces surprises. Daniel, in the poem of that name, is not of special interest, but our interest quickens at once when Belshazzar is called the 'wolf-hearted king'. This method of the gripped epithet (the noun holding another noun or adjective in a vice, so that it can't get away but shares its life with the noun and forms a compound name) is carried farther in Anglo-Saxon poetry than in any other poetry we are likely to know, and the poets never went to such trouble for nothing. The matters about which they cared are provided with gripped epithets, rich, striking, and (to us) new.

So that Anglo-Saxon poetry, then, did start off in a direction of its own. What in many poets would be, as it were, ornament 'tacked on', to the Anglo-Saxon poet was so essential that he could hardly manage a line without it.

The 'wolf-hearted king' actually takes the place of Belshazzar and is a kind of highly wrought substitute—a pronoun for Belshazzar. The poet skips on from pronoun substitute to decorative pronoun substitute, a string of copious condensed descriptions—'One word' (as the *Beowulf* poet says) 'finds another'. It is in *Romeo and Juliet* that Shakespeare ridicules the inevitable chiming together of certain words in love-poetry. 'Love' is bound to find 'dove' as a matter of course. A whole school of poets seemed to depend on such findings. In Anglo-Saxon poetry the clichés are of eagles who are eager, bravoes who are brave, ravens that are ravenous. The words which find each other and unroll as easily as a carpet are descriptive links. 'They loaded the wave-horses. Then they let the high ocean-dashers glide foaming over the monster-sea.' That must have been fairly easy to do: though there is much trouble and contortion in Anglo-Saxon poetry to express a transition of time or a shade of sentiment, the author of the poem on St. Helena takes the sea-voyage as an easy, traditional, effortless thing. He knows he can polish off the voyage with one hand held behind him, simply by using the best 'pronouns' for ship.

The reader will be interested to hear what success the poets had with such a method; but that must come later. It was certainly worth trying. With it they tried, as the reader probably knows, the method of systematic alliteration, instead of our modern arrangements of rhyme or blank verse. This is not so important for our purpose as the gripped-epithet method, in my judgement.

At the same time it is interesting to consider this method at work. After all, we have, as some writers tell us, the same fundamental language as the Anglo-Saxons, though theirs was apparently so different from ours. We have the same bold accents, landing with extraordinary fury on fixed points; but we have not now the same pure lingering sonorous vowels for the accents to fall upon. We have lost a number of the thick or splashy consonants, and we have added a number of little words nowadays, that patter along contentedly and get in the way or do their best to ensure that majesty and naturalness shall never in future join together in poetry. Long sonorous vowels and clashing consonants give the original alliterative effect, but we must never forget that this effect cannot be captured in modern English. What technique they employed is of no practical importance to us in this study, since if it makes a difference to that poetry it is a difference which the reader unlearned in Anglo-Saxon can never understand. It is idle to pretend that we can take the poetry apart from the language in which it is written. The language here offers certain possibilities which the poets are inevitably led to exploit.

13

The simple cross-gartered people who in the popular thought are the Anglo-Saxons did not produce simple poetry in the least. Their language was not easy to write in. The bulk of poetry they left is like a citadel to be assaulted. The poetical subjects are not ours—yet the difficulty is not so much a matter of subject, because a poet can make any subject interesting and affecting if he is a good poet—it lies rather in a fortification of uncomfortable words. Why the trouble to scale the castle wall? Why these incrustations on the fabric? If there are musical thoughts, why not offer them simply? These poets have not got musical thoughts; they have certain patterns to be filled out with few varieties of words. And by 'words' I mean words which stand for things each in their own right. An Anglo-Saxon word is as uncompromising as a table. Aloof, alone, solitary, not of itself suggesting company.

The few conventions of form suggest this. There is battle and seafaring, riddle and wise saying, the speech in high style, and the lament and lyric. When away from these forms the Anglo-Saxon poet is apt to be at a loss and drags his matter back into their patterns with apparent relief. 'Comrades', even in peace, are always 'battle-thanes'.

The difficulty of getting a striking half-line shows the limitation of form, to judge from the number of half-lines which are adapted from one poem to another. The same half-line is used in remarkably different contexts. It seems almost a point of pride and ingenuity to work it in, to alter it to suit the context. Which suggests a different method of working. There is first the difficulty of the extremely short segments. The fact that the sense has to stop at the end of the half-line gives you very little space indeed. It is extremely hard to contain it within that space. This is where their bold clashing epithets helped them, their fragments of hewn stone fitted into place. Like their armour, their ships, and their halls, their poetry was highly wrought, decorated with cunning work.

Together with their very different technique in writing, the Anglo-Saxons held a very different opinion from ourselves as to the form of a poem. The long poem maintained its grip on their literature, a fact which is unfortunate. No one cares very much now for epics, in however many books or cantos they are offered to us. Where Virgil is criticized and Milton scoffed at, it is not to be expected that *Beowulf* should escape, and even less, the long religious poems which make up so much of the bulk of the Old English poetry. Long poems seem to us to become a bad habit. The short Anglo-Saxon poems *do* maintain, on the whole, a high level which is not generally upheld by the long ones. In the long poems it really seems as though no one felt it necessary to be particularly effective in any one place.

'Plenty of room to be effective later on', the Anglo-Saxon poets seem to say. They have a habit of appearing to lead to a climax and then disappointing us. Nothing could be better, for instance, than the beginning of the poem on St. Andrew, with the Saint's reluctant voyage into the land of the cannibals, as he journeys guided by a helmsman, who, unknown to Andrew, is God. If we know much of Anglo-Saxon poetry, we shall be prepared for disappointment, and sure enough, there is little imagination in the rest of *Andreas*. I propose to give up the bulk of these religious poems, for the fragment of *Judith* is rather an heroic adventure. Two long poems, however, must be studied by the modern reader. They certainly supply that 'something different', so prized by us. These two are *Beowulf* and *Exodus*. *Beowulf*, in spite of tiresomely long harangues on foreign history and wearying displays of politeness, has a grandeur which comes through even in translation—a more sombre, curtained grandeur than anything the reader is likely to know. *Exodus* is frankly extended to a long poem by means of padding, but the padding (a matter of description *ad lib.*) is so astonishing in itself that we must certainly not neglect this extraordinary poem.

The shorter Anglo-Saxon poems are very attractive. The *Battle of Maldon* (p. 27) is the best battle-story which has ever been told in England. No one has denied its supremacy in its kind; though in this case it does not seem as though Anglo-Saxon poetry *does* show itself to be different. On the contrary, it seems to have shown us once for all how battle-poetry must be written.

There are the Riddles, not in the least like riddles as we know them, like that on the Moon and the Sun (p. 51) or the one on the Bookworm which gives away its answer— at the first word (p. 51). There is the Gnomic poetry (p. 49), much like the old Welsh poetry and far more remote from the ordinary than anything yet mentioned.

Finally there is the complaint or lament. This is the monologue of a person placed in a given (generally appalling) situation imagined by the poet. The *Wanderer*, the *Seafarer*, the *Wife's Plaint*, the *Husband's Message, Deor*, even the plaint of the Cross in the *Dream of the Rood*, the plaint of Satan (which is the best part of the later *Genesis*), the plaint of the father for his son on the gallows (in *Beowulf*) all show some characteristic of this curious form. It is the most interesting side of Anglo-Saxon poetry.

A strong ethical interest pervades most of the poems. They are thoughtful and generalized by reflections. Among the minor inducements to read foreign poetry or poetry in a dead language is the possibility of coming across a new set of values, quite different from our own. Chinese poetry, for instance, says Mr. Waley, sets friendship high and does not recognize love. This is one of its freshest appeals to our sophisticated taste who have set love on high for centuries, but when we want a poem of friendship have had for centuries to recall the bond of David and Jonathan from a literature very old and very different from our own. Is there anything in Anglo-Saxon literature of that kind? Can we see, as in the Chinese, some different turn to the relation between one man and another?

The Anglo-Saxon view has an angle of its own, recalling again in the moral sphere the gripped epithet. It presents a fusion of friendship and loyalty, patriotism and patronage all in one. We may see in the poetry how the friend and lord (gripped together in one compound word) is the centre of Anglo-Saxon sentiment. Ethical interest is centred in the friendly lord or the lordly friend. Even in the religious poems there is as much of this variety of friendship as there is of what we ordinarily regard as Christian feeling. Moses is the friendly master of the Hebrews. Christ is friend and master to St. Andrew.

Again, old poetry is read to recover some picture of old times, to inquire whether daily life was different or to trace the sameness under the difference and to sigh, 'plus ça change, plus c'est la même chose': 'Welcome is the dear sailor-man to the Frisian wife, when his boat is anchored, his keel, and her man, her own provider, is come home. So she summons him within, washes his dirty coat and gives him new clothing, and grants him on land what his love requires.'

.. Long is the sailor on his journey
Yet always expect him
The dear man, and wait, because no faster can he float
Till the wind comes round—he will return if he live
Unless the deep deflects him and the ocean has swallowed his boat.

But this ancient poetry only shows us glimpses of the daily life of these people. It does not show us what life in Anglo-Saxon times was like, so much as what the Anglo-Saxons would have wished it to have been like. They would have been glad to think that later times would suppose their poetry to be a mirror of their life, but a contemporary would shake his head: for instance, an effort is made in *Beowulf* to display the life of a king in his gold-plated, sky-scraper hall, where he bestows treasures. Though some colour is actually lent to the magnificent description (in which everything seems to be made of gold) by the discovery at Sutton Hoo of a tomb almost as gorgeously provided, the passages in *Beowulf* are best taken as a glorification of old days, a looking-back to the golden age of memories. And can there have been so much mead as flows through the poetry?

In a great heroic poem the reader expects such magnifications and likes them. What he misses are the gentler figures—Nausicaa and her maidens, the game of ball on the shore, the baskets of washing. But *Beowulf* is carefully sustained on the level of heroic deeds, as if deliberately arranged so that no homely figures intrude. There are no maidens washing on the shore.

These poems are valuable, not (as the Sagas) for the pictures of life long ago but for the aspirations of long ago—the different ethic. For the Anglo-Saxon would have agreed that conduct is the greater part of life. Most of their poems are highly ethical, though not always religious. *Beowulf* has a regular homily within it on the duties of a prince, and numerous asides to the same effect. It has even been suggested that the real subject of *Beowulf* is 'How the good ruler should act'; which may be absurd, but more pardonable than the reader who thinks of the poem as a muddle of wild fighting would imagine.

The Wanderer, who laments rather well, and might have left it at that, is so preoccupied with thoughts of 'Why did I do that?' or 'Why did that happen to me?' that he sits apart in brooding mood and won't help the poet to conclude. He is too sulky to go on with the poem and the poet has to finish it himself. *The Seafarer* shows the greatest interest in conduct. The *Battle of Maldon* is full of it.

Like primitive poetry much of the Anglo-Saxon poetry is anonymous. We know of three authors. There is

Cædmon, the cow-herd: he wrote a hymn of Creation which we have, and a long poem called *Genesis* has been associated with his name. Both have historic interest, but neither is important. There are also King Alfred and Cynewulf. The former turned the metres of Boethius into poetry; the latter wrote long religious poems, colourless and not distinguished.

At the same time we feel strongly that Anglo-Saxon poetry is not like ballad-poetry in being so primitive that it does not matter who composed it. Much of the poetry shows a high artistic self-consciousness and skill. Often one finds oneself wishing that one knew something about the poet who is taking so much trouble (in *Beowulf* or *Exodus*) for one's exhilaration. On the other hand, the critic who considers that he has elucidated a poem when he has shown it to be written on the day before the poet's wife died is here utterly foiled. It is not entirely foolish, this wish to know something of the author. It supplies us with a background, 'the lives, stories and acts of men', and if we remember that it is only a background, we may find it very helpful. Many of the most successful critical observations on literature of every kind are written when the critic is talking of something which, strictly considered, is irrelevant to the poetry, or at arm's length from it, like the poet's biography. But in this early poetry we must forgo that. The critic of such poetry must perforce write of the poetry and what the anonymous authors have left us in their lines of verse. It is in showing what the poems themselves are like that my translations are meant to be helpful. They are intended as part of the criticism, or if the poem really differs in translation I can warn the reader in what respects it differs. They will suggest, at any rate, the impression each poem makes on me. The comparative method is very useful in all literary criticism, but some of the best things in Anglo-Saxon poetry are unique. There is nothing to compare with *Beowulf* or with the *Battle of Maldon*.

From another point of view, we might suggest that Anglo-Saxon poetry should be studied because we *are* Anglo-Saxons. It is a curious thing that most English people know the Sagas of Iceland (or at least what a Saga of Iceland is like) far better than they do a poem of Anglo-Saxon origin. Yet, unless they come from York-shire or Cumberland, they are probably of the same blood as the author of *Beowulf*. Race is an enduring quality, and traces of the Anglo-Saxon outlook and expression seem still to linger among us. Contrast the fluency of the Celtic stories and of the French which came in with the Conquest with the restraint in the description of adventure which characterizes the Anglo-Saxon, the reticence in speaking of oneself, given as a principle in the *Wanderer* (though not observed in *Beowulf*), and the selfish humour of understate-ment. These are as characteristic of the modern English as of their ancestors.

Courage appears with splendid emphasis. We should like to claim it as English courage. Mr. Desmond MacCarthy has said that he draws strength of heart as he sits in a shelter with bombs falling round by reading of the utter heroism in Icelandic Sagas. These people will go on fight-ing when there is not the smallest possibility of victory.

The corresponding Anglo-Saxon Saga is the famous annal in the Chronicle, of Cynewulf and Cyneheard. 'And they were fighting until they all lay dead except for one British hostage and he was very badly wounded.' Or the famous speech of Byrhtwold in the *Battle of Maldon*, where the old man exhorts his company to hold fast in the losing battle:

> The will shall be harder, the courage shall be keener
> Spirit shall grow great, as our strength falls away.

Yet the same people are told,

> Foolish is he who does not dread lightning.
> Foolish is he who does not dread God.

If this is to be my own apologia for Anglo-Saxon poetry, I ought to add that I am attracted to it because I like the language itself and think it suitable for poetry. At first the language seems rough and uncouth. It has a cornery craggy look and its consonants seem to occur in thick groups. We come on a line like this,

> Oft Scyld Scefing sceathena threatum

which sounds something like 'Oft shield shaving shooters threatening' and remember our objection to cacophony. I have never been able personally to feel the ugliness, the cacophony, which it is asserted pursues poets with a 'bad ear'. Collins, for instance, has a line,

> With short shrill shriek flits by on leathern wing

which is also something like 'oft Scyld Scefing sceathena threatum', and thinking of such lines Johnson says that Collins's poetry is clogged and impeded with clusters of consonants. Then we are told that Tennyson took the utmost pains to smuggle his sibilants out of his poetry if he could. It seems to me to be labour wasted.

It is the vowelling of a line, far more than the bundling of the consonants that makes it sound good or bad. A thousand things have to be considered in poetry. There is the requirement that the line should be a pleasant variation from its predecessor; that the syntax should fit naturally into the space to be filled; that the stresses of the line should support the meaning; and when all these requirements are fulfilled it would be worth considering whether certain consonants or clusters of sounds which are thought cacophonous may be rearranged (especially the *s*, *sh*, *th* followed by other consonants). The Anglo-Saxons seem unaware of this cacophony, yet they pay very careful attention to vowelling and many of their lines are heavily sonorous:

Ālēdon thā lēōfne theoden

which sounds something like

Āll lāīd him dōwn, leader thrōnéd.

It is the strange consonant combinations of which we have no specimens in modern English which seem to us savage and uncouth. For instance, *wl* at the beginning of a word —*wlanc*—which seems as odd as the *ng* at the beginning of some African words—'Ngami'. Or *sth*, *shth* at the end of a verb. Actually *wlanc* (pronounced with its *a* far back) is a splendid word for its meaning, which is 'proud'. We have felt the advantage of having such a word in modern English and have conscribed *swanky* from one of the

23

dialects. *Wlanc* is a more serious word, but with the good elements of *swanky*.

So that Anglo-Saxon is a nice strong vigorous language for writing poetry. The words are stony and have character, and there is the great advantage in Anglo-Saxon verse that it is impossible to be neat. The short poem of *Deor* (p. 62) is the only poem in the language written in stanzas with a refrain. A refrain, one would think, must inevitably be neat. But instead we get the enigmatical

þaes ofereode, þisses swa mæg,

which was translated by Pound, 'That overpassing, this also may', flat and sprawling and not neat at all, but good. The Anglo-Saxon poets are well free of the tyranny of the epigram, the insolence of the paradox. Such constructions are a puzzle to them. Even in the Riddles they sprawl the language rather badly. The sort of ingenuity in the poem of the *Phoenix* after Lactantius baffles the Anglo-Saxon mind:

Mors illi Venus est, sola est in morte voluptas
Ut possit nasci, appetit ante mori;
Ipsa sibi proles, suus est pater et suus heres,
Nutrix ipsa sui, semper alumna sibi.

'Still to be neat, still to be dressed', was the end of this Latin poet. We can unpack the Latin into unpointed English.

Death is his bridal bed, pleasure consists all in Death,
That he may be born he lusts to be dead;
He is his own offspring, his own father, his own heir,
His own nurse, his own infant.

Now translate the Anglo-Saxon:

'He does not mourn his death, his sore killing, who always knows that there will be life renewed after his burning, a life after the destruction, when bravely in the manner of a bird he will be raised again from the ashes and will be young for ever under the roof of the clouds. He himself is both son and kind father and equally the heir once again to his old possessions.'

The attempt to sift good from bad in Anglo-Saxon poetry is beyond the scope of this cursory essay. In the selection of poems for translation I have been guided by the principle of choosing only such as have the Anglo-Saxon outlook, disregarding those which have only the ordinary medieval outlook, e.g. *Elene*, *Juliana*, *Guthlac*—all at a dead level of similarity. There is a fallacy in supposing that (as in the Ballads) a late poem must be inferior to an early one. As a fact the *Battle of Maldon*, which is certainly a late poem, is better than anything in Anglo-Saxon poetry except *Beowulf* and the *Seafarer*.

THE originals of most of the poems translated here are in Henry Sweet's *Anglo-Saxon Reader*. The rest, viz.—*The Fates and Gifts of Men, The Whale, The Song of Deor, The Wife's Plaint, The Husband's Message, The Ruin*—are preserved in the great tenth-century miscellany called the Exeter Book. *The Seafarer*, with its introductory note, was published in *Medium Aevum*, 1934, iii. 1. pp. 1–6. *The Happy Land*, which begins the book, translates a passage from the Anglo-Saxon poem on the *Phoenix*, and this version first appeared in *The London Mercury*.

The Battle of Maldon[1]

A.D. 991. *K. Ethelred's reign*

. . . got broken.
He made each warrior lash free his horse.
He bade them rouse the old might of their hands.
This the son of Offa took for a token
Of the courage-prick of that whole force.
(Their cowards would be put in bands.)
Therefore this chief let the hawk fly wild
To the open wood—which he bore on his wrist.
Now might a man know that he withstood
The foes of his lord as long as he could.
The lad would weaken not nor desist
When once he had taken his way
To the fight with weapons embroiled.

Edric, too, would help that day,
And ere the levy began
To stride forth with broad shields flung on them,
He was roused for battle-play.
Performing the boast vowed to his lord
To defend him to naked death.

Byrhtnoth too sets his array
Of warriors and inspirits them with his breath.
Riding and advising, he heartens the horde,
Tells them how to stand their ground, not give one inch away.

---

1 The metre of the original is rough and often defective. The MS. is no
longer extant, and was defective at beginning and end.

When he had rightly prepared them, this lord
Lights off his horse and stands among his people
Where he loved best to be—
Among his troops of dependants and hearth-horde.

Suddenly there appears on the bank a messenger of the Vikings and he
Shouts his errand over like a taunt from the other side:
'Bold ocean-men have sent me on before!
Find gold if you wish truce! Better it is for you
To buy off this inroad with riches and rings
Than that we should clash in war, and armies two
Should lose their blood. If you are rich enough, that brings
Long peace which we shall hold fast. Let the chief of your men
Give to the seafarers such money as they shall choose,
Then we shall call truce and begone again
In our ships over ocean. It is you who have all to lose.'
But Byrhtnoth the Earl as he clashed his shield
Finds it light to refuse.

'Robber, hear thou the answer we yield!
This people will give you no gold, but a spear,
This people will give you sharp shafts and new fear
And the long sword *you* cannot use.

Say then to your sea-chief this desperate thing:
This unconquered army stands firm with its lord
Who will protect their land, the land of Ethelred the King,
The place and the people. Hate wither the heathen horde!

Shall our people, our nation, bear
You to go hence with our gold? you that have come so far
Unfought with, into our country, carrying war!

28

Think you to get tribute softly and fair?
Point of spear must try it and grim battle-line.
Not a ring we resign!'

With that shields are taken up and men are ordered to go
Till they stand on the East bank.
Yet now the water begins to flow,
Neither can come at the other rank.
They thought it long until battle could be—
There the two armies bestride the stream,
The Flower of the East Saxons and the Rulers of the sea,
With the tide-lakes locking slow
And neither can hurt the other—
Unless a flying arrow laid some warrior low.

Then out goes the tide: the raiders stood keen,
Watching the water that rode between.

Now the Shield of his People set at the ford
A man tried in battle, Wulfstan most bold.
He killed the first man with his sword
Who plunged into water—with this son of Ceola old
Were two other fearless soldiers, Elfhere and Maccus,
Who never ceased to hold
The pass but doughtily withstood
As long as they could wield weapon that day.

But when the unwelcome strangers understood
How those bitter Ford-guards spilt their blood,
They begin to draw back and ask for free way
To come up from the mud.
Then the Earl in recklessness

Is prone to give too much room to the damned brood,
And was seen to call wildly over cold water
That son of Byrhthelm (all men heard what he cried):
'Now space is opened, come up quickly
And join new battle: God will decide
Which side is the victor and which sinks in slaughter.'

But the invading wolves care nought for the giver—
The whole troop plunge west over Panta river.
Lo! the rovers stand on the nearer side!

Yet the Earl and his army untroubled rest,
Form the phalanx with shield against breast
And wait for fight. Now was battle nigh
And wild war ready, and men were to die.
And the raven hears the foemen's voice
And the fat carrion-eagles speed and rejoice.
File-pointed flies the foreign spear,
Shaft against shield-wall shot and sped,
Wulfmere o'erwearied was wounded near
The brother of Byrhtnoth, once brave—he is dead!

Proud pirates perish.
I heard how, in haste,
Disdainfully, Edward drew
His sword to strike, and slew
And laid the line waste;
For this the thane thanked him
When a meeter moment came.
Steadily men stab the strangers;
Each man remembering him of the mighty fame
And glory in good striving.

Well the warriors wield
Unshivered shafts,
Arrow and shield.
They bore it bravely, for Byrhtnoth the thane
Breathes out daring, to daunt and abash the Dane.
Till a pirate prepares a prying lance;
Grim and fell does it glide
Quivering, to wind and glance
Into Byrhtnoth's breast, through his armour of brass.
He shook with his shield till the shaft sprang wide—
Angry was he, and eagerly struck
That proud pirate, and made a pass
Which got through his guard and ended his luck.
The Earl laughs, and thanks God beside.

But a foeman flung a further dart
So subtly that it struck again
One Ethelred's eager thane!
By his side stood a sturdy boy
Half-grown, who gallantly
Pulled the spear from the princely heart.
He was Wulfstan's child, young Wulfmere;
He sent the sharp shaft sailing back
With the tip truly trained, till he lay dead
Who had wounded the Earl, and caused our wrack.

Swiftly another armed man attacks the Earl
To relieve him of his rings and rain-patterned dagger.
But Byrhtnoth still bore a brown-edged brand
With which he could wound this warrior in the head
Till one of the seamen stopped his stroke.
Then the fallow-hilted sword slipped down on the face of the land,
Nor could he clutch the keen blade more.

Still the old warrior strikes out sturdy words,
Bids his band go bravely as before.

No force has he now to stand fast on his feet.
He looks to heaven:
                              'Lord I thank Thee
For all the pleasures I have plucked from this place,
O mild, though Mighty, I have now most need
To ask that my soul may sojourn safely with Thee—
I entreat that the pains of hell may not pierce me.'

Then the heathen hounds hewed him down
With both the brave ones who stood beside him.
Elfnoth and Wulfmere both lie dead
Who lost their life for the love of their lord.

Straight those turned from the strife who would not tarry—
Odda's son was the leader in flight—
Godric; forsaking both glory, and that good man
Who had so hugely honoured him with gifts of horses.
He stole away on the steed which was his master's
With the royal trappings in which it was not right he should be seen,
Both his brothers bustled away with him
Godric and Godwy, graceless, unregardful of glory.
They fled from the fight and flung into the forest
And more men with them than was meet—
When I bethink me of the benefits which the Earl had bestowed
On all his followers—As Offa said long ago,
'Many men boast mightily as they spill their mead
Who have no pluck to perform deeds at proof'.

Now the protector of the people being laid low,
Ethelred's Earl—all his army

32

Saw that their dear lord lies stark dead!
The proud men who press on, pray only
That the life in them may be vanquished, or their lord avenged.

Elfwine, son of Elfric, urges them on
Yearning after glory, though young in years:
'Remember how we rallied each other in the wide room
Where we met at mead, making each man
A bigger boast than his brother of the wine-bench,
Uncountable things. Now we can single out who at test is keen.
I will pledge for my ancestry—I am grandson of Aldhelm,
Made in Mercia of mighty stock.
He was wise and an Elder and ambitious in the world.
Therefore thanes of Mercia shall never cast an evil thought at me
That I fled from a foughten field
Flying to seek safety now my loved lord lies lifeless.
Hewn by the hands of heathen—Hateful it were to me
For he was my cousin and king.'

Then he flies forth so ferociously
That he spits one on the point of his spear
And bears him to the ground, by that emboldening them
His friends and fellow warriors, to fight unflinching on.

Offa cries, flinging up his ashen spear:
'Now you have heartened them, Elfwine, as our army requires:
When our Earl is fallen to earth, it is for us each to aid
With brave and willing words, as long as he can bear his weapon
Shaft, spear and sun-sharp sword. For surely Godric,
Odda's cowardly boy, has beaten us all
By stealing the battle-horse spread with kingly armour—
Men thought it must be our most worthy master
Who fled—therefore the field is made forceless and faint.'

Liefson laid on lustily, shaking the linden-shield aloft:
'I pledge my word not to withdraw the pace of a foot—
For the sake of my Prince now will I press forward.
At the town of Sturmer, no man shall call me traitor,
Saying that I lounged home without my lord.
But sword shall wind round me and weapon wound me
And I shall lie dead.' Thus did he despise cowardice.

As he charges, Dunnere, undaunted churl
Of commoner stock, yet begins to shout above the clamour
That every man shall avenge Byrhtnoth—
'He must not be in two minds, nor make a great matter of losing life
Who plans to avenge his master.'

So they rushed forth counting not their lives,
Hardily they held it out, the whole host.
Grim and bloody, they groan to God
Craving from him vengeance over a vile enemy.
Even the hostage helped us heartily.
(He came of brave kin in Scotland.)
Ashferth, son of Edgelaf, ably he aimed his arrows.
Some struck shields, some pierced soldiers,
Every now and then he killed one of their men.

Also Edward Longshanks is left among the living,
Boasting bravely not to budge a foot.
Singly he shattered the strong wall of shields
And worked wonders till he had worthily wreaked vengeance.
And so fell. Not far from him fought Ethelric,
Sibert's brother, and so did many another.
They cleave the keel of the shield and keep keenly on.
Offa strikes a seaman till he sinks and stretches himself asleep

And Gadda's cousin is graved in ground;
Quickly then is Offa's self hewn down by the host.
Not without deeds he had vowed to his prince
When he vaunted and not in vanity
That his lord and he should both gallop at last
Whole to their home or else be heaped among the slain.
Dying of wounds on one day
He lay nobly near his lord.

At last the shield-wall stood broken. The men of the sea burst in
Angry and aiming eager spears.
Often a lance pricked the life-house
Of a soldier who had been doomed long.
Wistan sallied against the warriors
Waging war by guile.
He killed three out of that throng
Before he too lies crumpled among the carnage.
That was a stiff struggle, but soldiers stood steady.
Many a man met his match being weary with wounds.
Oswold and Eadwold all the while,
The brothers, do bravely on the battlefield
Keeping their comrades stalwart through all,
Telling them how to stand the tempest and last out the dance.

At length rose Byrhtwold, lifting his shield,
An old retainer. He rears a lance.
With a passionate heart he holds his people—

'The will shall be harder, the courage shall be keener
Spirit shall grow great, as our strength falls away.
Here our lord lies, mangled and struck dead,
A good man prostrate: all his life shall he lament

35

That warrior who flies from this battle-death and glory.
Aged am I, yet I will not turn at the end
But was born to lie dead by my patron,
So dear a master—'

Also the son of Ethelgar summoned them all,
Godric was his name, to new feats of fierceness
Often he sent a spear veering into the Vikings.
Ever he went first, feinting and fighting
Till he lay spent of life on the lost field.
(It was another Godric who feared and fled.)

Judith

A Fragment

... SHE doubted not
The comfort of God in this wide world,
For ready was protection at the Ruler's hand
When she needed most—For her belief was secure
Ever in the Almighty. ...
                    Then Holofernes planned
His summons to the drinking—bid men make
Dainties most marvellously—bid all his band
Come—and they did, for their master's sake,
The rulers of the people:
That was on the fourth day since Judith,
Beautiful as a fairy, her path to him did take.

  So with rare heart to the banquet all men pressed,
Big to the quaffing of wine, that stern band
Who had helped in his ill-doings with armoured breast:
There were deep cups borne down the benches by many a hand,
And stoups, whole flagons brimming where they sat and made cheer,
Those strong warriors doomed to be dead
(Though their mighty leader had of this no fear,
The dangerous master of men). Then Holofernes dread
Was blessed at the pouring of wine—laughed, yelled and played,
Till the children of men could hear far and wide,
Exultant and overbearing with mead, how often he monished and bade
Those on the benches to bear themselves well, and finish each cask
    at their side.

37

So the vicious man up to the evening hour
Drenched his noble troop with wine from many a bowl,
Till overdrenched they lay in swoon, loosed of all power,
As given to death—drained out was every good trait of the soul.
Still they filled to those who sat, by order of the king,
Till night and the shades were on them. Then, devilish, scummed
    out of ill,
He says that the blessed maiden decked with many a ring
Shall be brought to his bed quickly.—At his will
They brought her: servants to the guest-room went
Where Judith, clear of mind, is found,—and bring away
The bright maid to the high tent
Where the master rested him alway;
The nightly cabin of our Saviour's foe
Holofernes!
        There was all golden and fair
A curtain hung round the bed, that the evil being might know
Who came into the chamber, and look on him there,
Though the incomer could not see, unless he were bidden near
To impart counsel.
        To the couch they brought soon
The wise lady, then went to tell their lord
That the holy woman had been taken into his inner room.
Now he felt big and luxurious, for he meant to distain
And smut with his filth the bright lady; but God, Judge of Glory,
The Ruler of Hosts, willed the man from that to restrain
And alter the story!
So, child of the devil, this man of lustful frame
Strode on with his guards terrible to that bed
Where he must lay down his glory and great fame
Quickly within one night—and lie dead.
(He endured upon earth a miserable doom

38

As he earned for himself, living under the clouds with men.)
Straightway he fell so drunk on his litter down in the room
That he knew no counsel in the box of his wits!
                    The watch began
(Wine-thick men) in a hurry to slip away;
They had guarded their lord to his bed—for the uttermost time—
For the handmaiden of God has in mind how best she may
Take the spirit from him, ere he wake, impure, to crime.
The virgin of the Lord, with platted hair,
Drew the blade from the sheath,
Began to name the Almighty in her prayer
And these words she saith:

'Lord of Creation, and Spirit of Comfort,
And Son of the Almighty—will I pray
For Thy mercy to me in danger,
Strength from the Trinity put forth.—For this day
Sorely is my heart aroused, heavy stored
My breast with sorrow tormented—O give me, Ruler of the skies,
Success and true belief, that with this sword
I may cut down this dealer of crime.—Grant me to rise
To salvation, O thou great Lord of men—
Never had I more need of pity now;
Carry onward to finish, O Lord, what is so grievous within
Upon my heart, and hot upon my brow!'

Now the Highest Judge lent might, as He doth to every man
Who asks with true belief. Then she gripped fast
By the hair the heathen man, dragged him on,
(Ignominy for him) and cast
Where she could reach him—Struck with shining sword
And severed half through the neck;
He was not dead.—With courage still

A second stroke she struck.
At that the foul body of the heathen hound
Was parted from the head, that rolled forth on the floor,
And the soul goes under the hollow headland, bound
To the fires of hell for evermore.

What manifest glory in the feat
When Judith, as taught by God, taking the creel
In which her white-cheeked servant had carried meat,
Brings back the head in a basket!
                                    Forth they steal
From the invaders' camp, till the ashen ramparts show
Of the city Bethulia; they haste where their steps had trodden,
Till they reach, light of heart, the gate in the wall
Where the soldiers sit and watch, as clever Judith had bidden.

And so to her people Judith was given again!
Bidding the gate be opened, loud she cried:
'What is worthy of thanks I tell—ye need no longer mourn in pain,
For the Lord is bountiful to you. Far and wide
Fame will arise among nations under the sky
That instead of trouble glory is yours this day!'

Happy were men in the city to hear her cry
Over the lofty wall. They hasten, and they
Throng and jostle, and in knots they run,
They press and they join round the maiden of the Lord,
And lo! she with the golden rings bids be undone
The head of the chieftain, bloody with the sword;
She made it as a signal to the throng
How she had fortuned in battle. And she said:
'Here may you who have victory see what we hate so long,
The heathen captain Holofernes' head!

Of all men he was the best at hatching murder
And breaking our hearts with sorrow—he would have tried
To bring us to worse despair—but God no further
Let him live to afflict us: through me this night he died
With the help of God.
                              Now shall your band
Take up shield and spear
To save this land,
For when eastern dawning is here
They are doomed—as God showed through my hand!'

     Then the troop was made up, gallant and stout,
To war at once; good comrades strode along
Soldiers and nobles bearing standards out,
They went to the battle due onwards all the throng,
With helmets from the holy city's self
Just at the first of dawn; their shields are sounding as they go
And speaking loud.—At that the meagre wolf
Was happy in the forest; so was the dark crow,
The bird that likes dead meat; both well knew
That the men meant to give them their fill of gutted things:
And behind them the eagle, ever hungry, flew,
With brown coat and water-dabbled wings,
And beak of horn, to sing its battle song. . . .
The warriors to the combat strode
With hollow shields upon them—men who long
Of foreign insult bore the load:
Keenly was that repaid at the javelin-play
To the Assyrians, when the Hebrews' host
Attained the field of battle.—Quick they launch away
A shower of arrows out of horn-bows loosed,
Like stinging snakes of battle—many a steady shaft—

And they give their cry, angry men of war,
And send spears among the enemies. Those homeland people chafed
Against the hated nation, sternly stepped before,
Brave of heart—not gently they surprised
Their ancient enemies who were tired from the mead;
They drew their bright-bladed swords well-tried
Out of the sheath, and struck the first who lead
The Assyrians, in earnest. High or low
They spared none of the army (their thoughts were full of hate)
Or left alive whom they might overthrow.

   So the kinsmen thanes in the dawning hour
Pressed the foreign soldiers all the while
Till the invaders' captains see the power
Of the Hebrews' swinging swords.—They went to make it known
To the greatest thanes among them, and endued
Those chiefs with the tidings—the sudden news is shown,
The morning horror to men in lassitude
From mead of the night. Then at once I heard
Those doomed to be slain broke from sleep,
And in little companies they stirred
Where the terrible master his special tent did keep,
Holofernes. They had in mind
To tell their captain how came the onset
Before the bitter Hebrews they should find
Come about their ears. For they thought yet
That the captain of armies and the maiden bright
Were together in the tent so proud of show—
Judith the noble and the man of lust and spite
And terror. Yet there was none dared go
To wake the soldier or to disclose
What he had done with the holy maid,

The virgin of the Lord.
                         The forces were drawing close,
The Hebrews fought in earnest with weapon unafraid,
Paying in the struggle their old grudge with brilliant sword;
The glory of Assyria was cast down
With that day's work.
                         Round the pavilion of their lord
Are standing soldiers, bold, foreboding in their heart.
Then all began to cough, to make a noise,
And gnash their teeth, men without God,
Expressing anger with their teeth; then were their joys
Dismissed, and all the glory in which they trod.
They thought that they would wake their lord—
They succeeded not!
                         Late and very slow
One of the soldiers was so assured
(A man of courage) as into the tent to go:
He discovered, thrown down white,
His master on the bed, soulless there,
Quit of life. In a moment at that sight
He fell to ground, all cold; began to tear his hair,
And rend his vesture, struck to the heart,
Crying these words to the soldiers of troubled mien
Who stood without: 'Here is shown a part
Of what follows for us—the time is almost seen
When we shall lose life as one
And perish in battle: Here lies cut with swords
Our master beheaded!'—
                         Then they threw down
Their weapons—weary-hearted turned away
To strive for flight. In their tracks men fought apace
Whose might was great, till the best part lay

Sacked in the battle, in that victorious place
Pleasant for wolves, or birds that like dead meat,
A comfort to them. Who lived fled away,
And in their tracks a troop of Hebrews fleet
Honoured with victory—for the Lord God that day
Had helped them well.

        There was leisure to take for reward
Bloody spoil out of their ancient foes,
Armour and trappings, shield and broad sword,
Brown helms, rich mountings.—For a month they came with those—
Helms and daggers, hoary corselet,
War-works for soldiers cusped with gold,
More skill-made treasures than any person yet
Could describe, to their bright stronghold
The city Bethulia—

        All that they obtained,
Those keen soldiers under banners at the fight,
Through the wise advice of Judith the brave maid,—
Whom to reward they took his sword, his helm in blood,
And the wide corselet furnished with gold that was red,
And whatever Holofernes had of treasure or heirloom good,
Rings and bright treasure—all that by one accord
They gave the maid with thankful heart!

        But for it all, Judith said
Thanks to the Lord of Hosts, who gave her the reward
And fame on earth—and reward too in heaven,
In eternal glory, because her belief was secured
Ever in the Almighty.—Verily at the end she did not doubt
The comfort she had hoped so long.—For which, to the Lord,
Be glory for ever, who made wind and the lift,
The heavens and wide earth, as also cruel streams,
And the joys of Heaven through his mighty gift!

The Fates and Gifts of Men

COMMONLY it happens (God help) on earth
That man and woman bring by birth
Their child to life, and give him his content,
Succour and foster, till the time is spent
As years are passing, when each young limb
And living members grow big with him:
So mother and father lead and carry their own,
Give to him and get for him.—But God alone
Knows what is to happen when the years have run,
And he grows up. . . .
                    In childhood-time for one
The ending to them who weep
Is pitiful.—Him the wolf shall eat,
The grey loper over the heath;
For his death the mother weepeth
Which is beyond men's control!
    Of one, hunger has toll;
One shall the rough wave wreck,
One shall spearman get,
One shall war destroy,
One shall keep still his life, though blind,
Fight his way along with his hands:
One shall find no movement in his feet,
Sick in the sinews—testy at his bands,
Upbraid his fate, afflicted is his mood.
    One from a high tree in a wood
Falls down, not having wings,
And yet he is a-flying—into the air he springs,

Till he has done with his attempt to be a fruit:
Then he tumbles down to the root;
Hopeless of life, he falls to ground,
His soul gone from him!
                        One man shall be bound
For distant countries by necessity
And carry his food with him on the way
Treading the weeping path to a hated land.
He has few to entertain him, and
The refugee is hated everywhere
For his misery.
                        One on gallows there
Shall ride to death, swing till the spirit's pen,
The bloody chest of bones is broken. Then
The Raven steals away the sight from his head,
The black-coat fellow slits him when he is dead;
He cannot prevent the crime with his hands
Which the enemy from the air does to him. Life gone,
With no feeling, pale on the bough, he shall wait on
For his fate, in a mist of blood,
His name is accurst!
                        One man is pursued
With a great fire of furious flame,—
Perilous over the doomed man it extends,
Red cruel fire.—How swift death came!
His mother weeps, who sees the brands
Cover her son!
                        From one, the edge of the sword
Takes his ale-sopped life at the board,
A man who has had enough—
He spoke too quickly!
                        One is carried off

46

By mead, while he sits and drinks,
From a server's hands. What he thinks
He cannot hold, or stop his mouth:
He shall lose life both
And joy—get what is worst of all,—
'Self-murder' they call,
Reproach in words the drinker's bout!

              By God's help, another shall work out
All his troubles when he is still
A youth—and in age shall do well—
With days of pleasure, riches many,
Goblets with his kindred to enjoy,
And wealth as great as any
Man alive can keep, and never cloy!

      For God variously gives destiny to every man—
Wealth to one; to another, distress;
Happy youth to one; happy battle to one,
Power at the sword-play; or success
At shooting or throwing; skill with the dice,
Tricks of the chequer-board; or some even grow
Clever writers; one has a special grace
At goldsmith's work, hardens and decks it so,
As he serves a leading king, that he gains
Broad lands from him for thanks, and likes them well:
One shall give pleasure to many thanes
As they sit at table with their ale,
There is the merriness of the drinkers great.—
Or one shall sit harping at the feet
Of his master, getting gain,
And ever cleverly pluck the strings back,
Set the plectrum that goes leaping, singing again,
The limber nail; his keenness, his attack

Is marvellous. One shall tame the strong
Haggard bird, the hawk upon his fist,
Till that fighting swallow is gentle; he puts on
Its jesses, and in its bonds he feeds it as he list
With meagre rates, till the Peregrine,
Proud of its feathers, humbler grows
To the man who feeds it, in its garb and mien,
And trained to the young man's hand.—So wonderful
The Ruler of Hosts the skills of men bestows
Through the earth to each one of our kind
Whose destiny is mighty. Let each say thanks
For all that to man in mercy He has assigned!

Gnomic Verses

Woes are catching: clouds are fading.
If you should ever advise a great lord,
Urge him to giving and not to invading.

A stream must mingle with the sea
And a mast stand tight when winds are free;
A sword be dear to humans still
And the wise serpent live in a hill;
A fish in water spread its race
And a king give gold from his lofty place;
An old hungry bear walk out on a heath
And a river fall over a hill without death.
An army united by unity stand
And truth be in man, and wisdom in his hand.
A wood cover the land with its courtly green boughs
And a hill be fresh green; and God in His house
The judger of deeds; and a door in a hall
Shall still be the wide mouth that opens to all,
And the shield have a bow where the fingers can lock.
Birds shall speed up to heaven from every tall rock,
The salmon shall leap like the shot of a bow
And showers bring discomfort on worldlings below.
A thief still steal out on the darkest of nights
And the Fiend live in fens full of misleading lights. . . .
God alone knows how He bestows
After death's day the souls of those
Who must seek judgment from His Face.
The future is dark and secret and the place

Where the victorious ones have set their throne
Was never seen by mortal, never known
To any who could set the matter so
That we are bound to believe, as much as awed to know.

Riddle on Moon and Sun

'I saw a creature sally with booty,
Between its horns bearing treasures amazing.
'Twas a bright cup of the air, a brave, pipkin-thing
Adorned with delicate, darting rays.
This plunder gay for a bower it would take
Spoil of the air, to its palace dim,
And, cunning, would build a room of its own in heaven.
Over the wall an arrogant being
Sprang up, though common to all men's sight is he.
He snatched the booty, drove the other home,
Wisp of a pilgrim; and westwards itself
The cruel creature went careering on.
Dust blew up. Dew came down.
The night followed after. But never a man
Knew where the wandering thing had gone.'

Riddle on the Bookworm

A moth ate words. That seemed to be
A curious matter, when the wonder dawned on me,
That a grub could eat up the words of a man,
A thief in the dark his teaching and plan,
And the stealthy guest
Would be no wiser for his eating of the nest.

51

A Charm against the Stitch

Against sudden needle-pains. Feverfew and red-nettle which grows into a house by a cranny, and dock, boil in butter.

Loud were they, loud, when they rode in a cloud,
They had but one mind, when they rode in the wind.

Save yourself, that this evil may disappear:
Out, little spear! Out, little spear—
If you're still stuck.

When the Fates ran amuck,
Those mighty old hags on their green-crested nags
Pressing horribly near, and couching their spear,
I stood under cover and darted one over,
An excellent arrow, its aim was so narrow.

Out, little spear,
If you are in!

A smith sat, he forged a forcing-pin,
He hammered the iron, and tempered and tried.

Out, little spear,
If you are inside!

Six smiths forged a bar out clear,
Out, little spear!
Why, you *are* out, spear!

If anything iron's got under thy pelt
The work of a witch, it shall melt, it shall melt!
If you were shot in the skin
Or the flesh or the blood or the limb,
Let it never hurt thee one atom
If it were a shot of a hag or of Satan
Or the shot of an elf, I can fetch
Something useful against an elf; something useful against a witch;
Something useful against a devil—I give you my skill!

Flit away by dusk woods to the perilous hill!
Be whole! may God help thee, omnipotent will!

The Whale

To explain the nature of fishes in craft of verse—
And first, the Great Whale. A grim purpose is his;
Mariners often find him against their will
Floating on eternal ocean.
His name is Fastitocolon,
His coat is like rough stone,
Like a huge sea-knot of wrack, ringed with sand-dunes,
That floats by the shore.
　　Now when wave-borne men trust their eyes for an island,
And moor their high-beaked ships to the fraudy shore,
Tether their sea-horses at the brink of ocean
And roam up the island to explore:
While the keels lie at the tide-mark
The tired sailors make their camp,
They wake a fire on the island,
Happy are the men, and tired—glad to encamp.
But he is crafty and treacherous; when he feels
The travellers properly planted and set
Taking the pretty weather—
　　　　　　　　　　　　　　Instantly down
Darts the oceanic animal,
And locks drowning in the hall of death
Both ships and souls!

54

The Dream of the Rood

I HAVE tried, in translation, to keep the metaphors in their strength. *Treow* I call 'tree', though the latest editors of the poem hint that the metaphor was so familiar to Anglo-Saxon ears that the transferred sense of 'cross' is best. They explain that *treow*, *beam*, and *gealga* all mean 'cross'. But surely *treow* is not here used in the literal meaning of 'cross'? It is used rather in the sense of 'tree' as a metaphor for 'cross'. A metaphor, like a human being, begins dying as soon as it is born.

At the risk of making a too striking effect in modern English by literal translation of what would be a commonplace phrase in Anglo-Saxon (like the translator from the Portuguese who said Charing Cross Bridge was 'the colour of the blood of an ox'), I prefer to regard these metaphors as living. It is only meant to dawn on the reader by degrees that the poem is about the Cross. This is proved by the line 'This was no malefactor's gallows', which comes after the description of the object as *treow*, *beam*, *beacen*. If these words had already given us to understand quite clearly that it was the Cross, to add later that it was not a murderer's gallows seems feeble.

Beacen, then, I call 'beacon', though it is true that the word has more meanings in Anglo-Saxon than our word *beacon*. It can mean 'emblem', 'sign', even 'vision'. The dreamer sees an extraordinary tree, a bright stem of wood surrounded by light. It seems like a beacon. Then again its glory has vanished. (The dream is changing, like the mists of a valley; the dreamer has not yet focused the apparition.) So that, though *beacen* may mean 'emblem' or 'sign', modern English so tends towards the abstract that to make any effect one must be very concrete. The word 'beacon' is concrete, and after the description of the radiance of the tree, where is the difficulty in translating 'beacon'? As metaphors for 'cross', these three words *treow* (tree), *beam* (stem or trunk), and *beacen* follow on one another with rich effect in the poem until the brilliant shining cross is the beacon of Christ. In fact, the author will call this vision in the sky anything but a cross that the effect may be heightened, when at last the word *Rod* is used. The delay in using the actual Anglo-Saxon word for 'Cross' is deliberate.

The jewellery of the Cross has been a difficulty to me. Modern taste desires otherwise, and I have tried to coax poetry from this, by thinking of the thin wafers of gold, so thin as to be almost spiritual, which a book-binder will waft on to the edges of precious books; 'gold to aiery thinness beat' laid with careful hands upon the Cross.

With the Cross still speaking its own sorrows, notice how suddenly, with an equally swift change of style in the poetry, God appears and tries to climb the Rood. The leisurely complaining of the Cross is broken into by the urgent God and urgent tragedy—Christ, the brave captain is swift.

The horror of the tree in its helplessness mounts steadily in the poem. Three times the desire to fall down and finish everything is repeated against all canons of art:—the first time rather cumbrously, the second more urgently. Then come two lines as final as a Latin epitaph. Excited details come before, and excited details follow after. These two lines, so curt and plain, seem to have the severity of graven stone:

> Rod wæs ic aræred—ahof ic ricne cyning
> Heofona hlaford: hyldan me ne dorste.

Later the poet builds well on this hard core of the poem—on the paradox of the Almighty wounded by mortal men. The men are more insignificant than is usual in passion narratives. The Cross and the Christ are vivid. The men do this or that. They are not stressed. Men? I forget them. Almighty God suffered through them and upon my body. So the Kenning *reord-berend*, at the beginning of the poem (which is in this case imaginative and not descriptive) has a significance from the tragic altitude of the Cross. It conveys the word 'men', but saves time in catching hold of the particular handle which is wanted in the poem—man as the disturber of silence.

> Lo, I will tell you the best of dreams,
> What I dreamt at midnight
> When men with their voices were at rest:

> I thought I saw the strangest tree
> Climbing the sky, wound round with light:
> The brightest shaft in the world,
> A beacon drenched in gold;
> A wonder of the night!

56

Gems shone fair on the earth below
And there were five jewels up on the shoulder-bough:
All the angels of God, eternal in beauty,
Behold it now.

O this is no gallows for a thief condemned
For good men on earth look thither with love,
All this created wonder, the world, sees it,
And the holy spirits above.

It is a tree of victory blazing on me
And my sin is foul before it:
I am wounded with infirmity:

I saw the glorious sign
Honoured with vestures, blissful shine,
And there seemed as gold cast o'er it,
And gems decked worthily the Ruler's Tree.

But beneath all the gold
I could see the trace of an old struggle and sad
When the right side sweat blood—O my heart swelled with trouble,
I was afraid of that glistering thing!

Then the swift beacon changed its glory,
Lost its fair look. I saw it stream cold,
Running with sweat of blood.—Then again it was a treasure
Of chosen gold.

So I lay there with ruth in my heart
On and on, watching the Healer's tree,
Till it spoke! Till I heard that most precious wood

57

Sound words in the silence:
'It was long since: they hewed me low
(But I remember!) in the forest-row.
They plucked me from my rooted heart,
Strong enemies, and by base art
Mismade me in a shape of scorn
And bid me swing their knaves unborn!
On men's shoulders I rode at last
To a little hill. Foes made me fast

Then I saw the Lord of man
Press on to climb me!
I dare not bend against command
Of the Lord, though I saw the land
Quiver and shudder in its clay.
I could throw down all his foes,
But I hold fast.
                              Heroic, fair,
This young knight who was God made bare
His breast. He was ready then,
In the sight of many, to ransom men.
He climbed the gallows, and he gave
No second thought, being sure and brave.
I shuddered when he clutched me round;
Flinch I dare not or fall to ground:
I was raised a cross, and it was I
Who swung an Emperor gallows-high:
The Lord of Heaven;
I durst not bow.

They drove dark nails through my side,
Open wounds of malice that abide

To be seen upon me. I durst not spurn
Our foes mocking us with hate and scorn.
I was wet with blood fallen from the man's breast
When soul went out, a wavering guest.
On that little hill I have overlived and borne
Cruel deeds. I saw stretched out and torn
Woeful, the Lord of Hosts.

Darkness has masked the failing day,
Our Healer's body, bloodless clay
Stretched on the gallows, the weak rain
Wraps round and hides. This world of pain
With all creation, cries its loss,
The fall of a king:
Christ is on the cross!
See, come from far, each man of good
Draws near the prince. And I, the Rood,
In sorrow, humbly to the sod
Bowed down. They took Almighty God
Out of hard pain. Limbweary lay
His corpse fallen on earth. But they
Stood at his head and beheld God
Who rested, lying spent after the great fight.
Before my sight—his slayer's sight—
They shaped his coffin of brightest stone.
They entombed the Lord
And in dusk, sorrowful,
Raised a mourning song.

They left me steamed with sweat,
With arrows hasped, with wounds o'erset:
We three stayed weeping
For his body, fair house of life grown cold.

We were hacked down—
Thrust in a pit. But his disciples found me,
His friends—In silver they wound me,
Wrapped me in gold.

Now canst thou know, O man beloved,
That all travail and bitterness have I tried:
Now the time is discovered
When men, and this famous wonder, the world, shall honour me full
    wide:
They are praying to this sign. On me God's Son
Suffered once; therefore now with might
I tower up under the heaven, and will work my healing on
Any of those who know fear in their heart for me:
Once did I go under hard spite
And the worst that can be inflicted—until I restored
The way of life to men, as it was right!
    Lo, the Ruler of Glory honoured me
Over all the trees in the forest, even as did the Lord
Honour His Mother Mary, where many see,
Above all kind of women. Beloved, I require
This sight thou relate to men,—unwrap for me
That this is the tree of glory, on which tree
God suffered for the many sins of man
And Adam's ancient works till judgement-day.
But through the cross must each soul part
From ways of earth, who hopes to live alway
With the Lord.' Then I prayed with happy heart
Zealous to the tree, where I was, all alone;
My mind was stirred to take the course from earth.
Hours many of longing have I known:

Now my pleasure of life is to repair
Oftener than all men to the wondrous tree
And serve it well. To that is the desire
Strong in my spirit, and my comfort is
Only from the cross. Few friends have I on earth;
From the world do they depart to find their bliss,
With the high Father they live in Heaven,
They stay in glory,—but I look still for the hour when this
Cross, which on earth by vision once I saw,
May come to me in the life that fades and dies,
And bring me then where is pure bliss,
Where the people of the Lord sit to feast—that I may rise
Where I may stay in glory, with saints of heaven,
To have joy. Be my Lord my friend,
Who here on earth suffered, even
On the gallows-tree for the sins of all mankind:
He redeemed us and gave us life,
A heavenly home.—How great then was the bliss
When the Son came victorious in His power
With all good souls, into God's domain,
And angels ever in glory—when their Master came,
Almighty God, where His kingdom is!

The Song of Deor

WELAND knew sorrows in his Wermland days,
Unflinchingly lived through a helpless maze,
And knew for comrades hardship and despair.
Cold wrack of winter exile stretched him there,
Ever since Nithhad robbed his knees of strength,
And cut each sinew till he crawled at length;
    That passed, as this of mine may do!

The murder of her dearest brothers two
Was not so hard to bear for Beadohild,
As her own hap, when finding she was filled
And pregnant with the burden in her womb,
She could but think upon her growing doom.
We know from story that this hurt she knew.
    That passed, as this of mine may do!

The Gotha grieving for his children knew not sleep,
Sorrow unmatched would leave him but to weep;
    That passed, as this of mine may do!

Theodoric for thirty winters drew
His breath in exile, underwent the fall,
Common to men and sorrow known to all,
    That passed, as this of mine may do!

We know the history of Eormanric,
The Gothic king of wolfish strength, who stained
The country of the Goths with blood. Tyrant he reigned,

While many a man in secret nursed his smart,
And wished a steel were buried in one heart.
   That passed, as this of mine may do!

As a man sits, cut off from pleasure's view,
It seems to him as though the stretch of ill
Which lies before him, mounting like a hill,
Is endless. Let him call to mind, our God
Descends and visits even the lowest sod
And visits it with joys or else with pains.
Now let me tell, that once my famous strains
In harping and in poesy were known,
In Heodening's hall was Deor's skill best shown.
For many winters I held high esteem,
And a true lord—till now when most men deem
The better singer is Heorrenda new.
   That passed, as this of mine may do!

The Wife's Plaint

THIS song I make of my own heavy heart
And the plight of my life—I can say
What hurt me since I grew to be a woman,
Of old and new—more than ever to-day;
Always have I fought with many cares.

First my true-love went away
From the leaping strand:
This was my grief in the dawning,—
Where was my master, where his happy land?

Then must I go too, to find some hand
To help me, friendless creature, in my dearth.
But then began the people of his kin
To plot in their secret thoughts how to keep us two apart,
So that, sundered the furthest of any on earth,
We should live most like enemies—I was sick at heart!

After this my love—unkind—said men should take
And put me here—in this place,
Where few dear ones or any friend have I,
And sad is my fate
To find a man who was mine—my own mate—
Stern in soul, go heavily
Covering his mind, practice to show his cruelty!

How often we two vowed with happiness
Nothing but death could divide us—death divide!

That has o'ertaxed itself—for now our bliss
Is gone as it never were. And far and wide
I must go beneath his anger—loving him who does this!

Men bid me live in the forest boughs
Under an oak-tree in the earthen cave:
Old is this earthy house; my heart is broken!
There are dim valleys and steep high hills,
Bitter fortalices made of briars,
A joyless place. Here often the pang is mine
Of how my husband left me. . . .—Lovers' fires
Are warm on earth—one bed for two—
When in the new-woken twilight I pace away
Under the oak-tree through these earthen caves,
Where I may sit through all a summer's day,
Where I may weep through all a summer's day
My hardship and misfortunes bitterly,
For never have I peace from all the care of my life
Nor the broken heart that came to me!

Henceforth my young lover shall be but sad,
And keen the reproach of his heart, however gay
His look appear; and weight will come down
Upon his soul for ever—both if his joy
Is at his hand, or if, hunted out,
Far from his nation it is that my lover sits
Under slopes of stone with storms that shed frost,
Pitiful master of mine—water round about—
In drear house. Perhaps my lord suffers
Grim care of mind, too often remembers a throng
Of blissful places. Alas for those who must
Wait for the beloved with aching heart so long!

The Husband's Message

HERE am I fresh from the barque,
From long wandering free.
Thou shalt know the dear love of thy lord,
For he says it in me
That thy faith may repose on the truth of his word.
See! he graved in this bough,
And bids it bring to thought
The hours when gold-bedecked you heard his vow,
Ere feud had wrought
His exile and your parting at the end—
Bright hours when, love scarce grown, you stood his friend.
Hear then his charge to thee:—
When the first cuckoo's throat
Sends shrilly its sad note
At the edges of the sea,
Set out and stir the wave,
Let no man stay your vow,
But climb on the shoulder brave
Of a ship with a southerly prow,
To seek beyond the sea-gull's home
The joyful man who waits there till you come!
He has conquered all his woes:
He will have no lack of steeds,
Of drink, joy, treasure; no foes;
But bright cups and glowing deeds,
And best of all, you, Princess, for his wife!
And often he mutters a rune.
Calling on Sigel and Wyn,

And swearing, if he has life,
(I have heard him) the very tune
Of those oaths he will hold to the letter
Once made by you two when the world went better.

The Wanderer

OFTEN the solitary man looks till God will bring
Pity and help.—But long on the ocean ways
He must sweep with his hands the rime-cold sea
By tracks of pain. Fate is a moveless thing.

So spoke a wanderer who feels old troubles,
Toil and lost battles and the murder of his kin:
'Often and many a dawn I must weep my sorrows
Alone—For none lives now to enter in
The locked door in the heart. Well the custom stands
As a good law for a good man
To bind fast his heart and keep those bands,
Think what he will. The charged mind little can
Against Fate, nor the ruined heart
Bear others' ills. Therefore those ambitious to be strong
Bind up each pitiless thought in the coffer apart.
And so must I in chains seal my heart too long,
My poor lean heart—since the shadow of Earth covered
My dear ready master of gold, and on the wave at the end
Heavy as winter I went under the thwart weather
Seeking unhappy the hall of some prince and friend,
Where far or near I could find one to know me
And comfort me left alone.—But he who has tried can tell forth
How bitter is sorrow for companion
To the man with not a friend on earth!
    The paths of exile bind him fast,
Not chains of gold—And chill at last
His breast, locked not with gold of the world.

He thinks of the hall men—how the booty was given abroad—
For in youth he was at feast with a golden lord—
But that joy is watched and done.
   The man who must alone forgo
His wise lord's sayings, dreameth so
When sorrow and sleep together bind
The poor heart singled from its kind;—
He thinks that as of old his lord
Is taking homage from the horde,
And that he mounts to the great place
To kiss his master and embrace
And lay down both hands and head
On his knee—for that life he led!
The lordless man then wakes and finds
The fallow sea stripped by cold winds
With seabirds sousing in the spray,
And the hail and the snow seep down day by day.
Heavier are the wounds then
For the sweet lord in his heart. And when
The sorrow of the thoughts of kin
Runs through his mind and searches in,
His heart goes to find them in the hall,
The warriors of old strength.—But they fall away,
His mind does not bring back to him many of their fleeting words.
So his care is renewed, as often as he lifts up
To travel over the water in its compassing cup
His weary thought.
                    Therefore, through all the world I cannot find
Why shadow should not on my spirit fall
When I scan through all the life of humankind,
How they suddenly left the hall,
The mighty kin of thanes.—So this world each day

69

'Totters down and falls.' . . .
A man shall have to realize how bad it will be
When what was pleasant in the world stands as waste
As now throughout the world those vast
Ruins stand, crazed with the wind, spread with rime,
Tottering bulwarks. . . .

The wine-halls linger to decay,
Their lord is taken from the pleasant day.
The flower of man is fallen down
Proud by the wall. War took its own,
And carried in its course to sleep.
A ship has borne one over the deep:
The hoary wolf one rid
To death; with sad look, man hid
One in earthy grave.—So the Ruler of humankind
Has punished this plot enclosed, till the cries
Of their inmates all brushed away
The houses raised of giants empty lay.

   But the man who wisely ponders on the place thrown down,
And scans this dark life with a frown,
Wise in his heart, shall remember from far back
How men have fallen, and these words shall speak:
   'Where is the steed? Where is the man? Where is the giving of
      gold?
The places of feasting? Where is the pleasant hall of old?
Alas for the bright cup! Alas for the man of war!
Alas for glory of princes! How the time goes o'er,
It vanishes under night's shade, as it had never been!
   Where the dear flower of men had lain
A wall stands shining under stain
Of serpents, wonderfully great.
The force of spears took men, and power of fate,

And the bloodstained weapon thrown.
Storms strike these cliffs of stone:
The coming blast binds the earth,
The roaring of winter, when the dark springs forth:
The shades of night are dropping athwart;
From the north it sends in men's hurt
A rough sally of hail.
All is hardship on the earth, and fails
What providence had set in the world under heaven.
Here shortly is wealth given;
Here, to have a friend is short;
Here, man is short; here, kinship short,
All the order of the world shall be in vain!'
   So spoke the wise man, and that was the train
Of his musing as he sat. . . .
Happy is he who keeps his faith: his anger starts not abroad
Till the sequel he can finish with his sword.
Well it is for him who looks for a merciful hand
From the Father in heaven, where for us all the fortress stands.

The Seafarer

THIS version of *The Seafarer* was made to bring out clearly the variety of mood which I find in the poem. In this respect indeed *The Seafarer* may be compared with the bastard Pindaric Ode of the eighteenth century, which afforded such a remarkable opportunity for the expression of a diversity of feelings. And this species of ode, which runs the whole gamut of emotions, is a defensible form—consistency of tone is not a poetic virtue, or has not been in England. Yet while Augustan anger, sorrow, or martial glory, kept in separate strophes, would always receive under Dryden's or Collins's hands a clear distinction of metre, the Anglo-Saxon poet suffered from limited measures, which went to disguise his rather similar intent. I have no doubt that *The Seafarer* is a poem in which one man is mixing his moods, and my version tries to make this plainer by forcing him always to a corresponding mixture of measures.

I have exaggerated any hints that are in the poem. I have shortened the short lines ending:

> . . . þæt ic feorr heonan
> elþeodigra eard gesece

and lengthened the long following lines:

> For þon nis þæs modwlonc monn ofer eorþan

to show that a new and vigorous impulse towards summing up the whole situation has fallen on the Seafarer, after his premature and self-awed wish to put out on the sea has died away. But he is always changing his mind, oftener than the metre shows it—for instance how he breaks off Elegy and gives three times a plunge towards Satire as he thinks of the landsmen—and that is the main attraction of the poem. I find it easy when I consider this to take the last sententious lines of my extract (I stop at the same point as Sweet) as but one more mood of the same man. Mere resignation to God may be a bad staple of poetry, but Wordsworth in *Resolution and Independence* found, like the poet who wrote *The Seafarer*, its poetic sufficiency for the close. Indeed, I was bound to continue the translation to the point where the crowded feelings come to a temporary halt. I did not feel willing, either, to abandon the earlier part of this passage, though it has been called

72

commonplace, and contains nothing about the sea. For the keen edge of something quite unanswerable disconcerts the reader in these lines as it had done at the very opening of the 'soþgiedd':

> ne mæg him þonne se flæschoma þonne him þæt feorg losað
> ne swete forswelgan ne sar gefelan
> ne hond onhreran ne mid hyge þencan.

It has not the piquancy to modern ears of an early and incompetent seaman, who hates his element, yet 'what shall supersede reality?'

An American critic, Mr. T. S. Eliot, in attacking Gilbert Murray,[1] suggests that a verse translator should at any rate not add material invented by himself to the words of his author. As Dr. Johnson is said to have consoled himself for the fact that he was not working on his edition of Shakespeare by the thought that at least he was not working at anything else, so I ought, I suppose, to console myself for the fact that I am not writing poetry like the Exeter Book by the fact that at least I am not writing poetry of my own. I do not, however, bind myself by the rule suggested. I have kept near the Old English when a translation seemed likely to produce the same poetical effect, but have taken liberty to invent in many places, attempting, for instance, to bring home to the comfortable reader at the outset the same feelings of

> Pain, hunger, cold that makes the heart to quake,

as the old poet, who wished to fret and sear indifferent minds. But words like 'breast-care', 'travail' will not do that in my hands, and the translator must try to put poetical acid into the words as best he can. I should conclude with the admission that in my kind of translation it is more important to produce poetical acid of the same formula than to preserve any strict equivalence of words.

> What I know, I shall launch in this stave—
>   Truth, from tired days.
> The trailing hours, toilsome and grave,
>   When the heart says:—
> 'All ships are keeps of care, islands of fear,
> In the heavy bright water!'

[1] *The Sacred Wood*, p. 67.

73

But night hid the clear
When we knocked past the cliffs—
   Strait was the watch of old
   Which found me at the stem in the pining cold,
   My feet chained down with ice.—But burning care
Boiled round my heart.—And hunger often files
Its way in flesh.—

            O, when a man finds fair
Fortune on the isles,
He has then no thought for these rime-cold
Sliding seas of winter where I spend
This exile and tract of life!—Dead is my friend.
Icicles hang around me.—Hail is flung in the air!—

   Only the crawling of the wave
      I heard, and the ice-bound surges die.
   Sometimes the swan would be so brave
      As, in her lonely way, to cry.

   I made gay thoughts out of gannets' notes,
      I held the puffin-bird could smile:
   The sea-mew was singing instead of the throats
      In the mead-hall, that beat up a ballad erewhile.

   Storms struck the stone-cliffs as the tern
      With dewy feathers screamed above.
   Over and over answered the erne
      With icy wings—
            No friend, no shelter of love
For the want in my heart!—
            So the burgher in lust
Who lives within great walls, engrossing joy,

Happy and high with wine—drinks and does not trust
This talk of sailing—
                              While I live, weary!

It darkens. From the North
The curling snow steals forth.
The frost is on the land.
A smallish warning band
Of hailstones falls in chain—
The coldest kind of grain!
And the thought knocks my heart
To tempt those deep streams!
Often in the day
My wish tells me the way
Over the sport of the waves
To far lands!

O no man is proud enough yet in the earth,
    So gifted of heaven, so young or so hale,
So loved by his God, or so sure of his worth
    That he does not fear danger setting to sail!
He wonders how heaven will treat him.
    He hasn't the pleasure in gold
Nor the heart for a harp, nor the joy in a wife—
    All the pastimes of earth are grown old—
He can think about only the rolling and strife
    Of big waves beating the hold—
So his heart is fed with longing, who wends to the blue and the cold!

The boughs take blossom, towns are gay,
    The meadows green, and Spring's in train:
All these things urge me on my way

To seek the lonely floods again
O vainly does the cuckoo sing
(The keeper of the gate of Spring)
Who pines my ear with her boding tone!

(A thing to happier men unknown
What exiles feel, who tempt strange ways
With danger!)
           As my mind turns back the days,
It leaves the breast, the locker-up of woes,
To cross the whale's wet country—yearns and goes
Where men live happy—comes once more to me
Drooping and sad—till the slow bird of the sea
That wheels alone, and presses me from rest,
Chides my ship on, to cross a new sea-crest!

The bliss of heaven is warm as a breath,
But this dead life is cold to my clay.
What Life thinks weal is brushed away
Greedily, after a glance, by Death!

Ere a man die, three things suffice
To bring him to despair:—
Age or disease or feud efface
His keen life out of the air!

The firmest track a man may leave
Is in the thought of his land:
Then let him bring the Devil to grieve
By the dear works of his hand,
That the children of men make a tale of him
And he hold heaven fast!—

But such deeds are fled, Caesar is dead,
Kings look best in the past.
Lordship is nothing to the old days
When men lived in loyal fame.
The flower is fallen, this is the stubble,
Weak men walk in a world of trouble,
What was noble runs lame!

The deeds that were glory halt out of our ways
Like each man in our province called Earth who grows old:
When age creeps upon him and powders his head,
The hoar-pate mourns that his friend is dead,
A son of the great—ready for the mould!

See then, the body, when the life is ta'en,
May not taste sweetness, may not sense a sore,
Or raise a hand, or reason with its brain!
And though a man should place a thing of worth
Early beside his brother in the grave,
It climbs not with that soul, but rots in earth . . .

Fear towards God is great, 'twas he who framed
The strong roots of the world, and the plains for men,
The leaning sky. A fool who fears not is shamed,
Death comes in a moment and nooses him again.
But the humble man whose belief is sure
God will help to endure.

The Ruin

A Fragment

CURIOUS is this stonework! The Fates destroyed it;
The torn buildings falter: moulders the work of giants.
The roofs are tipped down, the turrets turn over,
The barred gate is broken, white lies on mortar
The frost, and open stands the arching, cumber of lumber
Eaten under with age. Earth has the Lord-Builders;
The dust holds them while a thousand
Generations are ended.
Lichen-gray, pink shining, this wall lasts out
Empire and empire again, stands long under storms
Steep, deep,—only to fall!
The foundations with clamps were marvellously fitted together
By some brave man. . . .
Bright were the palaces, baths were set in the palaces,
Gables high assembled, there was the press of people,
Many a hall to sup the mead, so rich with joys for men,
Till time when Fate the strong rescinded that!
   For then they shrank as pestilence came,
Pest took their strong pride. As for their towers,
Their prime fortress was waste foundations,
And men who could restore it in a multitude fell down.
So these courts stand lonesome still—red vaulting, and that roof
With its curved frame that sheds tiles—drop, stop, drop—
Where many a warrior once, glad-heart, gold-bright,
Well-fed, wine-protected, in display of armour,
Could look on treasure, on silver, on subtle skill-knit gems,

On wealth, on worth, on coloured coats, on pearls,
On a bright city in a broad kingdom!
  Stone courtyards stood there, and a stream threw hot
Its wide repulse of water; a wall went round about.
Where the baths sit, with bosom bright,
Hot in the midst—facilitable enough!

        .   .   .   .   .

They let hot streams lapse over blocks of grey,
Circle-tanks . . . hot . . .
Where the baths were . .   It is an admirable thing!